MOMENTS IN TIME

A COLLECTION OF POEMS BY DARSHELL HINES

Copyright © 2001 by Darshell M. Hines

All rights reserved, including the right of reproduction
in whole or in part in any form.

For

My Mother

I love you more than you can possibly imagine. Thank you for life. Thank you for doing the best you could with what you had at the time. I know it wasn't easy raising your children on your own but job well done. Don't ever let anyone take that from you. Remember, you and God alone are the creation of me.

My Children

I am so grateful to have been blessed with all four of you. To have had an opportunity to share in your lives has helped me develop into the person that I am. Four distinct beings with four distinct personalities have taught me that each one of you is special and an individual gift from God. Because of you, I survived.

Thomas, you dwell in my heart, mind and soul. I love you with every ounce of my being.

Vanessa, thank you for loving me in ways no one but you could. You are the reason I live. Your unconditional love is irreplaceable. You are my best friend. I love you.

(Baby) Otha, my mini-me, you give me life. You give me reason to smile everyday, reason to move, and reason to do. You keep me from aging. I love you.

Damarcus, a lesson of faith. I am grateful beyond expression and my faith shall falter not. I love you with all my might.

ACKNOWLEDGEMENTS

God, thank you for loving me when I couldn't love myself. Thank you for Your gifts, talents, and creative ideas. Thank you for life. Thank you for Your coverage, redemption, and for answering all my prayers.

Auntie (Audrey), thank you for the years you gave, the love you gave, and all your moments of support.

Nina (my other daughter), thank you for coming into our lives. You are an integral part of our family.

Michelle, Libby, India, Laurice, Dayna, Adrienne, Gabby, Kevin, Gerard, Marie, Joi, and *Cheree,* thank you all for loving me and taking me as I am. You will always be my family.

Renee, thank you for your friendship and for believing in me.

Bruce, Tammy, Curtis and *Endisha,* you are never forgotten.

Anthony, words cannot explain the motivation, the inspiration, and the major part you played in one of God's gift to me. Thank you. You will always be.

Kimberly (my cousin), thank you for coming into my life.

All my other god children, cousins, nieces, nephews, aunts, uncles, friends, associates and anyone else I forgot to mention, thank you all for crossing my path. It is because of my experiences with you, I was able to write and publish this book.

To all of you, thank you

TABLE OF CONTENTS

1. My Friend
2. New Lover
3. Falling Too
4. Love Making
5. I Miss You
6. I Love You Darling
7. The Loneliness Of Another Woman
8. Long Ago
9. Letting Go
10. Wondering
11. A Lover's Apology
12. Goodbye
13. A Friends Apology
14. Soul Mate
15. Memories
16. To Love Someone
17. Cheer Up
18. Sister
19. Morning Pain
20. Silent Pain
21. You're My Friend
22. Speechless
23. My Boy and My Girl
24. My Love
25. Admitting To Love
26. Are We Going To Be Together Forever
27. I Couldn't Find The Words
28. Last Night
29. Now That You're Gone
30. You
31. You're More To Me
32. Longing To Hold You Near

Page	Title
33	Forbidden Love
34	Feeling Heartache
35	New Beginnings
36	Time That You Knew
37	You're My Everything
38	A Way To Say I Love You
39	My Love Before
40	Growing Past
41	Old But New
42	Holding On
43	Times When I Think of You
44	Immune
45	Smile
46	You May Never Know
47	As I Think
48	Yesterday
49	Dedicated To All
50	Letting You Go
51	If Tears Would Come
52	Hurting
53	Moments Spent Alone
54	I Thought Of You Today
55	Congratulations
56	Loneliness
57	Letting Go Of Love
58	It's Time To Change
59	When The Heart Won't Let You Go
60	I Might Say To You I Love You
61	Forgetful Love
62	Sorry For The Pain
63	Keeper Of My Heart
64	Detachment
65	I Must Have More Than One

MY FRIEND

Every time I need you;
You are always there;
Every time a tear drop falls;
You wipe away my tear;

Sitting home alone at night
When I get so depressed;
You take the time to listen to me;
It helps relieve my stress;

You need to know the things you do;
I keep inside my heart;
I hope that nothing but death alone
Will keep us two apart;

But if we go to heaven
And see each other there;
I know we'll recognize each other;
For the love we share;

Thanks for being my BEST FRIEND;
Although it is a task;
I LOVE you for it;
I THANK you for it;
I PRAY our friendship lasts.

4/5/94

NEW LOVER

Sitting at work
    Thinking of you;
        The kisses, the touches,
            The things that you do;

I daydream, fantasize;
    The love we share;
        I know in your heart
            You really care;

While lying in the dark
    Late at night;
        Your rubs, your holds,
            They feel so right;

The passion that's burning
    Inside of me;
        It's released in our
            Lovemaking energy;

Make love to me, caress me;
    Don't let it fade away;
        If you want me or need me;
            My love is here to stay;

Even though it's soon;
    You have won my heart;
        Take care of it, cherish it;
            Let it never depart.

4/13/94

FALLING TOO

I'm falling for you
It scares me away;
When I see you and hold you;
I don't know what to say;

I choke on my words;
But I want to tell you;
The feelings and emotions
I'm going through;

There's my tendency to want you
More and more;
It breaks my heart
When you walk out the door;

Then there are thoughts of love making
In my head;
I want to hug you and kiss you
Till we both drop dead;

On top of that
There are crazy ideas;
Hopes and dreams;
Wishes and prayers;

Although I don't know what
You've done to me;
It seems you've conquered my heart
Now it's no longer free;

It must have been God
From heaven above;
He sent you to me
For he knew I needed love;

Now that you're here
I hope that you'll stay;
Fall madly in love
And be happy one day.

4/13/94

LOVE MAKING

Kissing tenderly
Your lips all over mine;
We've been together
Dating one another for some time;

Caress me then lick me;
I think the time is right;
Make love to me and rock me
All throughout the night;

Start by blowing in my ears;
Whispering I love you;
Proceed to sucking on my chest;
I'll guide you through and through;

Kiss me on my tummy;
Rub me on my thighs;
It feels so good; the ecstasy;
I have to close my eyes;

Once we've released our juices
But before we start to rest;
I think you ought to know
That you are certainly the best.

4/14/94

I MISS YOU

As I think of our love making
    I miss you;

The way that you touch me
    It feels so fine;

Your tender kisses, the passion
    I miss having you near me;

Just to see you, talk to you
    You are so handsome, so beautiful;

Your smile, the happiness;
    I miss you;

Just the simple person that you are means so much;
    The things we share, the moments alone;

Stay forever, don't ever go away;
    I miss you;
    I'll miss your love.

4/21/94

I LOVE YOU DARLING

I Love You Darling,
  More than life itself;
  More than the sun shines
    On the hottest days;

More than it rains on rainy days;
  More than thunder;
  More than Lightening;

More than a thousand breathes in one breath;
More than a million tear drops;

I love you more than a billion miles of sea;
  More than all the land;

I love you baby,
  More than you'll ever know;
  More than you can ever imagine possible

Love Me

6/27/94

THE LONELINESS OF ANOTHER WOMAN

The kisses I want, I must wait for;
The affection I need is all given away;
The touch of my man's arms around me is temporary;
   Not forever;

When I turn in my sleep at night
   There is no one there;
No one to hold me, to love me;
Security is what I lack;

The smile he brings me, it easily fades away;
"I love you" is not heard or show in a fashion that I'd like;
The companion I need is not there;
I need to talk; I must call a friend;

The emptiness is always there;
   The fulfillment, never;
The moments can indeed happen
   But not with the one I love;
   For I am not first;
   I am second.

8/94

LONG AGO

Once ago I fell in love
The memory of my life;
Developed hopes had faith and dreams
That I would be your wife;

You brought me joy, plenty smiles;
Completed happiness;
We topped the moments making love
Then ending with a kiss;

Heaven lasted not so long;
Hell had found its way;
I loved you and I needed you;
So, I began to pray;

Confusion disappeared at once;
For God was on my side;
He wiped away the tears that fell
And carried me with pride;

He said, hold thee with loving care;
Never let thee go;
For If I stayed and worked it out
Our love could only grow;

I thanked the Lord for guiding me;
My life, I know I owe;
I love you now, forever more;
Just as long ago.

9/6/94

LETTING GO

Letting go of laughter;
      Letting go of dreams;
            Letting go of you
                  Is harder than it seems;

Letting go of smiles;
      Letting go of hope;
            Thinking and wondering
                  How I'm gonna cope;

Letting go of love;
      Letting go of wishes;
            Tender moments making love;
                  Filled with hugs and kisses;

Letting go of pain;
      Letting go of tears;
            Letting go of all the time
                  We spent throughout the years;

Letting go of anger;
      Something I must do
            Means letting go of us;
                  So I can make it through.

9/6/94

WONDERING

I wonder where I'm going to;
    A part of life I'm going through;

I wonder why I love thee so;
    What's in my heart you'll never know;

I wonder why we fight and fuss;
    Do we love each other or is it lust;

    Why we're in love, why we feel pain;
    Do you take me serious or is it a game;

I wonder why I need you near;
I wonder if you really care;

I wonder about a lot in life;
I wonder if I'll become your wife;

    Do you think of me sometimes at night;
    Is our romance wrong or is it right;

I wonder what tomorrow brings;
    No tears nor frowns maybe happier things;

To wonder is to think;
That's what it really means;
To wish and to hope;
To wonder is to dream.

9/21/94

A LOVER'S APOLOGY

I'm writing this poem to apologize, I probably hurt you more than I realize;
I love you more than you'll ever know, please stay baby, please don't go;
    I need you right here, right beside me;
You're the only one I love with whom I want to be;
    I was stupid and dumb, I made a mistake;
Now I can't go to sleep, I'm constantly awake;
    I want to go back to where we used to be;
Me loving you and you loving me;
    I'll take away the hurt; I'll take away the pain;
I'll hold you and comfort you; I'll take all the blame;
    I'll make up for it, I promise you;
I'll do anything you want me to;
    I promise to bring you smiles and joy;
All the hurt feeling, I intend to destroy;
    You're my sunshine, my flower, my lover, my friend;
Please say you'll forgive me it's not the end;
    Please try to understand, what I've been going through;
I honestly didn't wish to bring pain upon you;
    I'm now asking you for a brand new start;
And to accept my apology, it's from my heart.

9/21/94

GOODBYE

It's time to say goodbye my friend;
    This relationship of ours must come to an end;
Once a long, long time ago;
    I loved you more than you'll ever know;
Our happiness has turned to sorrow and my smiles they turned to tears;
    The joy that used to fill me has faded throughout the years;
We used to trust and love one another;
    Now neither of us respects the other;
It seems like everyday you're lying;
    I believed at once you were really trying;
Trying so hard to be sincere;
    I felt in my heart that you really cared;
Now I'm realizing the truth you see;
    You can't be honest so I'm gonna set you free;
You've hurt me once, you've hurt me twice;
    But hell would freeze over, it would turn to ice;
Before you can ever hurt me again;
    No, we can't be lovers and we can't be friends;
It hurts me to say goodbye my friend;
    It brings tears to my eyes to know it's the end;
But I can't take the pain of it anymore;
    It's time that I walk right out that door;
There's no turning around or looking back;
    It's time that I put my life on track;
So once again, Goodbye my friend;
    I will always love you but this is the end.

9/21/94

A Friend's Apology

I'm writing this poem to apologize;
I hope you understand and realize;
People hurt each other unknowingly;
That's a part of life unfortunately;
I have made a mistake, but we all do;
All I'm asking is that we pull this through;
I know you have put your trust into me;
I know I let you down but can't you see;
It hurts me to know that I have hurt you;
I miss all the things that we used to do;
I'll make up for all the hurt I have caused;
I'll make up for all the days that we lost;
Forgive me, accept my apology;
Cause that's what a friendship is suppose to be.

9/26/94

SOUL MATE

There are times when I want you more than you know;
    And I'm in need of you always but it might not show;

You're a special, precious part of my life;
    Remember before, I was to be your wife;

Remember the days when I carried your child;
    Remember her birthdays, remember our smiles;

Who could've known then we'd be doomed by fate;
    Our "so called" friends would throw us the bate;

Arguments occurred and fights then began;
    We left one another we said "it's the end";

Fate couldn't be stopped, we we're torn apart;
    I didn't know then it would hurt my heart;

I had all the answers; I knew what I was doing;
    Who was I kidding and who was I fooling;

My biggest mistake; I let you go free;
    Although I have a man I still long for thee;

No soul can replace our sweet memories;
    No soul can fulfill the things that I need;

People believe our bond isn't so;
    How in the world will they ever know;

Since you've been gone; I've been half, not whole;
    My days have been long and my nights have been cold;

When I think about us I can't help but dwell;
    Maybe someday you'll feel the same as well;

You're my life, my soul mate, you always have been;
    God will bring us back together before the end.

9/30/94

MEMORIES

*M*emories are precious
Memories are dear
Memories are thoughts
That last throughout the year.

*M*emories make us happy
Memories make us sad
Some memories make us moody
Others make us mad.

A memory may bring smiles
Remind us of those who care
A memory can bring hurt
And lots of painful tears.

*T*here are memories we cherish
Others we might regret
Some things in life we may remember
Others we might forget.

A memory is a need, a want
It also is a must
It's Gods greatest gift in life
That he has given us.

10/03/94

TO LOVE SOMEONE

To love someone is to care;
                       To always want them near;
To think of them always;
During nights and during days;
                       To cherish them the most;
To brag and to boast;
Stand by them when the going gets tough;
                       All through the good and especially the
       rough;
To stay with them through thick and thin;
Regardless of the price,
                       Their love you'll win.

                 10/94

CHEER UP

Cheer up lover, sweet baby of mine;
God wanted this to be a sign;
Maybe he wanted you to recognize me;
Maybe he wanted to set you free;

I'll bring you all smiles; I'll chase away sorrow;
Make your sun shine today, bring laughter tomorrow;
When pain is your past and you're feeling good;
I'll take care of your heart like a woman should;

Fulfill your dreams; make them all come true;
After today you won't be blue;
Kiss you and love you, give you my all;
We'll do it together; I won't let you fall;

Forget about the past; what used to be there;
Together we'll make it, your sadness we'll share;
So cheer up lover, sweet baby of mine;
God wanted this to be a sign.

10/10/94

SISTER

Sister of mine, did you ever guess,
You're a special part of me you are the best;

    Imagine the things in life that I do,
    I made it this far because of you;

You have stood by me through thick and thin,
That's the way you've always been;

    During days I felt I couldn't go on,
    You gave me strength and courage, you made me strong;

We argued and fussed, we pushed and shoved;
But deep in our hearts, we knew it was love;

    Through good times and bad times, happy and sad,
    You were still my friend when I made you mad;

Some friends may leave and you'll never know when,
But a sister is forever, until the end.

    10/94

MORNING PAIN

Morning sun; I woke up, no tears within my eyes;
Not long before the pain had set in and I realize;
You won't be coming back to me;
For her, this you will do;
Tomorrow will bring happiness or will I still be blue;
Will sun shine on my happy days and fill my heart with joy;
How could you hurt me like this man; you must be just a boy;
When love is found as strong as mine; you hold fast and you keep;
For no bond will be tighter than the love that falls this deep;
Who gave you all this courage boy, how could you even dare;
To hurt me and to walk away as if you do not care;
The teardrop in my eye will be part of yesterday;
This morning pain I'm feeling will surely fade away.

10/31/94

SILENT PAIN

Silent Pain distracts the sleep, in the darkness, tears I weep;

Silent Pain does one not care; it's the type of pain one cannot bare;

Silent Pain screaming inside, feeling betrayed, wanting to hide;

Silent Pain felt, not seen; remembering the past for what it's been;

Silent Pain cutting the heart, dealing with notions of being apart;

Silent Pain does anyone see the agony and hurt it causes me;

Silent Pain bringing me down, it's pulling me deep, making me drown;

Silent Pain burning my soul, an experience inside to help me grow.

11/2/94

YOU'RE MY FRIEND

*B*ecause you're my friend
I wish you were here;
Thoughts of a friendship
I hold so dear;

*W*hen I needed an ear
You loaned me yours;
You never had a reason
You never had a cause;

*C*arrying the problems of the world
Feeling like I couldn't go on;
You gave me both strength and courage
You proved me wrong;

*D*uring good times in my life
Both before and after;
It was you who filled my heart
With joy and laughter;

*Y*ou're a friend in my book
Something you'll always remain;
Cause during both good and bad times
It was you who came;

*L*ife hasn't been the same
Since my friend has been gone;
But with thoughts of our friendship
I'll carry on.

11/3/94

*Y*ou ask me to write you, nothing comes to mind;
So much happening, you're assuming I'm blind;
You want me to talk; I have nothing to say;
What difference will it make in your actions anyway;
In light of these actions, with nothing being new;
My thoughts are speechless, my feelings are too;
Know my not communicating plays no part;
I still love you for you're in my heart;
I'd just rather not talk, just keep it inside;
I'd rather not struggle with you to abide;
I'd rather not argue so here's the deal;
We'd get along better if my lips stay sealed.

11/23/94

MY BOY AND MY GIRL

The Lord hath given me a boy and a girl;
The greatest gifts in all the world;
Children that I may call my own;
Even when their older and fully grown;

He gave me first, a handsome boy;
He knew that this would bring me joy;
He delivered this in part you see;
Cause this would be the man
That would stand by me;

He would give me strength;
He'd be my back bone;
He would be the man to head my home;

Next, he gave me a pretty little girl;
Her smiles could brighten the entire world;
He delivered her to me for my heart she'd win;
To take care of her to nurture her;
To be her friend;
To encourage her in life so that she may succeed;
To hold her and comfort her in her time of need;

Regardless who may come in our lives we know;
That whether they stay or whether they go;
We'll always be bonded forever, us three;
We'll always have each other, we're a family.

11/3/94

My Love

My love, My love, My sweet dear love, you are the one for me;
My love, My love, My sweet dear love, you hold me tenderly;
My love, My love, My sweet dear love, I want to be with you;
My love, My love, My sweet dear love, I also need you too;
My love, My love, My sweet dear love, You're special in my heart;
My love, My love, My sweet dear love, I knew this from the start;
My love, My love, My sweet dear love, with whom I wish to be;
My love, My love, My sweet dear love, loving happily.

12/6/94

ADMITTING TO LOVE

It's been some time since we first met;
Now as time continues to go by;
My hearts beginning to feel some things;
Feelings I can't deny;

When you first came into my life;
I was all alone;
I didn't posses the happiness;
That every man should own;

You took away the loneliness;
You filled my heart with cheer;
I began to feel admiration;
And longed to have you near;

The times you held me in your arms;
The most precious times of all;
It was then I began to realize;
That my heart was starting to fall;

I didn't want to admit it;
I said it can't be true;
But I can't forget those moments;
No matter what I do;

Now I'm giving in to love;
Admitting that it's true;
I know that deep inside my heart;
I'm falling in love with you.

12/19/94

Are We Going To Be Together Forever

Are we going to be together forever?

Are these feelings I'm sitting here having normal?

Is one supposed to want another this bad?

Even if there came a time when the other may not feel the same?

Is there ever a point where one should say "forget it" and just walk away?

What makes one give in to, settle, or hold on to someone they only think is their "whole world"?

Life is bigger than love alone!

In the end, will one receive their paradise they tried so hard to seek?

What makes two different human beings from two different worlds bond and need one another such as we need each other?

Will this feeling of need alone, keep us two together?

Are we going to be together forever?

12/21/94

I Couldn't Find The Words

I couldn't find the words to tell you
  What I'm feeling inside;
I couldn't find the courage to describe
  My emotions I've tried to hide;

I couldn't find the strength to explain
  My not being able to sleep;
And, I definitely couldn't proclaim
  That my feelings for you are deep;

Maybe if I were to tell you
  The thought would push you away;
The fear of you rejecting me
  Has prompt my need to say;

I didn't want to scare you
  Didn't want to come on strong;
Didn't want to be demanding
  Seems we haven't been dating long;

Understand how much I yearn to hold you
  In my arms at night;
Understand a desire deep at heart
  One to make things right;

Accept the way I'm feeling
  For that will be a start;
Let our moments capture you
  And keep inside your heart.

12/28/94

LAST NIGHT

Last night made me open my eyes,
Holding you close, I realize
That although we have problems;
And we fuss and we fight,
When everything seems wrong
And nothing seems right;
Let us have faith in the love that we share;
And forget not how much the other one cares;
Always remember, the good times we spent;
We would have never made it this far,
If our love wasn't meant;
Let us see now, that our love dies none
And cherish it forever from this moment on.

1/11/95

NOW THAT YOU'RE GONE

Now that you're gone, I feel sad, I feel blue;
I mope and I cry, I'm lonely too;
Our love to me it meant so much;
Now I'm afraid and cold I miss your touch;
Why'd we come this far to just let go;
I don't understand, I just don't know;
Now that It's over for good this time;
And I'm no longer yours and you're no longer mine;
I'll take with me our happy times;
But I'll leave the sad behind;
For in those thoughts of happiness, the strength I need, I'll find;
I'll never regret what we once had;
Or what you meant to me;
Nor regret my loving you, for it was meant to be;
I'll make it through these hurtful times;
If you'll just be my friend;
For in time I know that my sad heart;
Will surely start to mend;
Happiness will come to light;
And although we're not together;
I'll still hold on to memories;
Of love with you forever.

1/19/95

YOU

First I met you
And that was when I realized
I wanted you;

Then I got you
That's when I thought
I didn't want you
As bad as I thought I did before;

Then I lost you
That was when I became devastated;
I thought my whole life was over;
I thought I died.

Then you came back into my life
And it was then
That I thanked God
For giving to me,
The best thing in all of life;
YOU.

1/20/95

YOU'RE MORE TO ME

All in life has not been sad;
  Nor has been paradise;
But to fall in love then loose love;
  There is such a hurtful price;

      To think I'd never live again;
        Be burdened with such pain;
        To pray to God for brighter days;
          To take away the rain;

To wish and hope for someone new;
  One to start out fresh;
To fall in love then loose again;
  For he was like the rest;

        To lose my faith and all my strength;
          To give up once again;
          To shed a tear and fear inside;
        My heart will never mend;

  To doubt there is a man indeed;
For me to love again;
  To not accept what's in my heart;
To call you just a friend;

          You've made me smile and also laugh;
          You washed some pain away;
            Since tomorrow is no guarantee;
          The time has come to say;

  You're more to me than just a friend;
I wish for love with you;
    I hope one day within your heart;
You feel as if I do.

LONGING TO HOLD YOU NEAR

I tossed and I turned in my sleep;
I needed for you to be there;
For, I woke up in the darkness;
With a longing to hold you near;

The ring cut through the silence;
So I picked up my phone to see;
But my heart was disappointed;
For, it wasn't you for me;

I looked outside my window;
To watch the fall of rain;
Realizing, to sleep without you;
There is a hidden pain;

Finally it hit me; loneliness;
So I weep;
I need for you to lie beside me;
So I can fall asleep;

I know you're still a part of me;
And there's no need for a tear;
But I wish you were beside me;
For, I long to hold you near.

FORBIDDEN LOVE

My forbidden love,
I love you;
I will always love you with all my heart;
What is it you've done to me?
Why is my need for you so great?
Why is there always pain and tears with you?
I dreamt of days full of laughter with you;
I dreamt of children, marriage, all smiles;
Happiness;
Why are you forbidden?
Instead of brining out the best in me, you bring out the worst;
You made me cry;
Not want to love;
You burned my soul, yet and still I long for thee;
I ask myself, what is wrong with me;
I receive no answer; just the pain of it all;
Again I say I love you;
I will always love you, but you are forbidden;
For, my happiness is more important than the pain I receive
loving you.

Feeling Heartache

I woke up with heartache
Searching for strength to guide me through;
For I reminisced back down the years
When my heart belonged to you;

*I'*m scared to turn each corner
And I'm afraid to sleep at night;
Wishing we were still together
When love with you felt right;

*N*o tears have come external
Though they flow deep down inside;
Pretending not to hurt
Emotions I must hide;

*M*y feeling all this heartache
Is not for me to know;
But to understand there comes a time
We all must let it go;

*S*wallow all the pain
And wipe away the tears;
Acknowledge that although we did not make it
There was no loss of years;

*T*o hurt and cry, there is no wrong
And heartache is no sin;
We all must suffer these emotions
To better ourselves within.

NEW BEGINNINGS

Falling tears and broken hearts
Have gone into the past;
For with a start of new beginnings
Our love will surely last;

Our rainy days will wash away
For brighter ones lay ahead;
Frowns we had will fade away
And our smiles will appear instead;

Where no one was there to hold on to
A new love has come to be;
To hold and love forever and more
To share life happily;

To kiss and caress, to wish and dream,
To respect and hope and pray;
To know there is a need inside
Of both of us to stay;

Looking ahead at new beginnings
And not reminiscing down our pasts;
We'll focus our strength on love with each other
And build our foundation to last.

TIME THAT YOU KNEW

I think it's time you know how I feel;
    All this love that's flowing inside;
My need for you and want for you;
    To always be by my side;

        Deep in my heart where I have been hurt;
            You take the pain away;
        You give me reason to smile again;
            And hope for a brand new day;

When you're away not by my side;
    I miss you desperately;
But I know you will be back again;
    To love and care for me;

        My dreams at night, they're all of you;
            And the love that we both share;
        I pray and hope and wish as well;
            Through eternity you will be here;

I like when you hold me and whisper you care;
    For there's comfort I feel within;
I like when you kiss me and love me once more;
    Over, and over again;

        I want you and need you;
            It's time that you knew;
        My feelings inside;
            For I love you too.

YOU'RE MY EVERYTHING

Darling, *I love you with all my heart;*
You mean the world to me;
You are the air I breathe each day;
You are my destiny;

You *are my hopes and all my dreams;*
You are my everything;
You are the one I wished for love;
My handsome Nubian King;

You *are my needs and all my wants;*
You are my happiness;
The one I long to love and hold;
You are the one I miss;

I *fall to sleep with thoughts of you;*
And dream of you each night;
You are the one still on my mind;
When darkness turns to light;

My *love for you falls deeper than;*
The deepest of all seas;
It's strong yet soft and gentle as;
An early summer breeze;

My *love will never fade away;*
Towards you, it will always be;
It is something guaranteed to last;
Throughout eternity.

A WAY TO SAY I LOVE YOU

I needed a way to tell you again
The words I often do.
I needed a way to tell you that
I'm so in-love with you.

Something sweet yet different,
Something precious for my dear;
A way to show how much I love you
Filled with tender care.

I thought and thought and thought
And I searched but could not find;
No ways, nor words that would describe
What's in my heart and mind.

After all my thinking
Of the words that I could choose.
There was no word, nor phrase in mind
To top the "I Love You".

So, now I'm saying once again
The words I often do.
But not nearly enough.
My darling, I Love You

MY LOVE BEFORE

*I want to say I love you
But I told you this before;
To let you know I love you
Just as much, but even more;*

*To tell you that the love I feel
The one straight from the start;
Has grown and grown and grown
And filled up my whole heart;*

*The times I used to spend with you
Was sufficient way back then;
But now I long for moments when
I'll see you once again;*

*Hugging, kissing, and quiet moments
Spent between us two;
Memories of such happiness
That's all I have of you;*

*You're more than special; I mustn't deny
You're more than a dream come true;
For all my seconds of all my days
Are spent with thoughts of you.*

GROWING PAST

Past-
    Sometimes come to present tense;
However-
    Life we find has changed us since;

    Joy and tears
        Our younger days;
    We've grown within
        To change our ways;

        Searched for new
            Left old behind;
      To find us in a change of time;

            Straight ahead
                No turning back;
            No search for things
                Our life has lacked;

                Engulf in new
                    Our bond holds tight;
                Protect and love
                    With all my might;

                    Begin to build a brand new life
                        With you my husband;
                And I,
                    Your wife.

            11/27/95

OLD BUT NEW

You were sweet and tender
  As you lay within my arms;
I kissed, caressed, and loved you
  Through the evening, until dawn;

I did not want to imagine
  All the time I lost with you;
You were in my life before
  But, I was so confused;

How could I let you slip away
  And not pursue you then;
To know the sweetness of your love
  I'm feeling now within;

I wish my past allowed me to
  Hold you once before;
But, now you're in my life again
  The meaning so much more;

Fantasies of future days
  Envisioned loving you;
A friendship brewed from older ones
  A courtship sweet and new.

HOLDING ON

Complications loving you
I begin to wonder what should I do;

Hold on to one that may not care
Suck in more pain I cannot bare;

Suffer in silence, weep at night
Argue, not talk to make things right;

Wishing for heaven but settling for hell
Accept in my heart it will never get well;

Hold on to dreams that may not come
Insist on being your only one;

Opportunities pass; as each go by
I pray to the Lord and ask him why;

Coldness, anger resentment too
Holding on to be with you;

Hold on to one I should let go
Afraid to let my feelings show;

Staying beneath not being on top
A part of us I can't adopt;

Should I hold on, it will make things worse
Seems I've realized I should be first;

Rise ahead; above all the rest
I know that I deserve the best.

TIMES WHEN I THINK OF YOU

There are times when I think of you
    And my heart, it knows why;
        I dream and reminisce of you
            As the days pass us by;
What we shared, love was special
    True love it was indeed;
        Now the moments have past us by
            But my heart is still in need;
I can't help but to wish
    That our love still danced on;
        Where did it all go
            Is it really gone;
Life it is a struggle
    As my days they past by;
        I'd give anything I could
            For you to be at my side;
I love you still darling
    Yes, I pray for time when;
        I'll be able to caress you
            In my arms once again.

IMMUNE

The heart becomes IMMUNE
 To feel it, to know it
To see the truth within
 Pins sharp with pain;

Why do you not understand
 I am IMMUNE;

All of the present has been my past,
 I have walked this journey not once but many, many times ago;

I am not sour for I am bright
 I can walk this walk in darkness; no light;
A blank mind; thoughts are not around; IMMUNE!
Why is it when I say this, you do not understand
 I am not hardened, I am IMMUNE;

It's quite alright, for
 I HAVE walked this walk before;

I say to you a game; you say no
 I know this is real, I've been in life before;
 Games end; life is forever, a journey we must all take;

Emptiness!
 A bottomless pit, deep within;
Alone,
 God has put us here alone; he has made it so that each of us can sustain aloneness;

I know I can endure; weakness creeps upon me,
 Sneaking, Tricking; I cannot take this journey by myself;
Focus!
Pray!
Meditate!
God has said I can!

8/99

SMILE

I smile a smile of yesterday;
Happiness has gone; She's not near;
I smile a smile of yesteryear;

A grin not smile displays my face; Endures the pain of here today;
Don't mistake, it's gone away; To suffer not for yesterday;

I must not say, she won't be back; For knowledge of that time I lack;
But as we're here, the present now; I know she's gone and don't know how.

8/99

YOU MAY NEVER KNOW

You were here, you were real and now you're gone
    It's amazing that I could have thoughts you may never know;

I may never see your face again
    I may never hear your voice again;

I may never know what it's like to lay on your chest at night again
    You may never even know I think these thoughts;

You may never know that I think of you
    You may never know that you're all that I am currently thinking of;

Scary to know
    I may have to live with all of these thoughts by myself;

How did I get stuck with such a chore?

Had I never let you into my life
    I would never feel as I do and

I would never be stuck with the chore of dealing with it.

1999

AS I THINK

As I think, I smile;
    To know you're here, my heart may rest;

My head still pounds;
    The weight is partially gone, but not fully;
Not until you hold me in your arms;
    Not until I see your eyes;
Not until I see your smile;

It won't go away until
    I am finally where I belong;
    Where I want to be;

In your arms holding me, never letting me go;
    Your strong embrace;
    Please settle my heart, let it rest with ease.

8/99

YESTERDAY

Yesterday did bring the tears
    To pass through life without you near;

To never know you'll be again
    To hold this pain, do cry within;

The settlement of my heart won't come
    To pass and live without the one;

To fight for it to not exist
    The memory of your tender kiss;

To want your love inside my heart
    To not imagine, we are apart;

To cry and hope and wish and pray
    To make exist not yesterday;

A need so deep, I want to share
    I rest at peace when you are here;

Love me, Love me, Love me dear
    To hold me tight and wipe my tear.

8/99

DEDICATED TO ALL

Dear Heavens
    Dear Children
    Dear Mother

Dear Sisters
    Dear Cousins
    Dear Brothers

Dear Aunts
    And Uncles
    Dear Best Friends Too

Dear Grandma
    Dear Grandpa
    And My God Children, You!

    I love you like no love before;
    It's great, it's strong
    It's fierce and more;
    It runs deep, it is my soul
    It's all of me, it makes me whole;
    My thoughts each day are thoughts of you;
    Your smiles, your tears
    Your laughter too;
    Life's no struggle because, you're here;
    You're special to me you are my dear;
    Every day that life goes on and on
    It's thoughts of you that keep me strong;
    You're a precious gift
    From God Above;
    The BEST gift of all,
    It is YOUR LOVE!

10/5/99

LETTING YOU GO

Letting you go is difficult, A hard task to achieve.
Setting you free to fly away, You turn away and leave.
My heart aches, and
The pounding of the throbbing deep within,
Becomes too much for me to bear
My eye released its tear.
It's hard to see you walking As your sun is shining bright.
I sit in total darkness
In my morning, noon, and night.

I know I should be smiling And be happy that you are.
And deep inside I want to be
I've let you go so far,
Now you're free my birdie And, I'll struggle to fly on.
I wish you total happiness
Now that you are gone.

6/5/00

IF TEARS WOULD COME

If my tears will fall upon,
My cheeks from inside out;
To release the tension deep inside
What is this pain about?

If my tears will help me feel,
The person that I am;
Please lord above help them come,
So crying that I can;

If my tears would come, I know,
How happy I can be;
To free my mind for brighter thoughts,
A future I can see;

If tears would come, the rain would fade,
The sun would shine bright;
Darker days would begin to change,
And suddenly be light;

If a river of my tears would fall,
I know it would fall deep;
The pain of all the hurtful times,
My heart has chosen to keep;

I need my tears to roll out and,
Release me from this jail;
Then I'll be free and,
All the ones that need to know, I'll tell;

Our tears are a gift from God above,
And it's natural to release;
An ocean of your pain inside and,
Find your inner peace.

6/6/00

Hurting

I whisper that I hurt inside
 The pain I feel within;
The scream of something drowning me
 Please forgive me for my sin;

Loneliness I walk at night
 No vision of a sun;
But when I rest my body down
 I know my chores not done;

Tiredness that creeps all day
 The mind won't take a break;
The throbbing of my heart inside
 The pain of my heartache;

Does this feeling fade away
 Does life begin to grow;
Am I to be destined to walk alone
 While both young and old;

Others sun is shining bright
 Causing them to blind;
The happy thought of living life
 Is nothing quite like mine;

Does it stop, and when will it
 Lift up from its toll
Bring me smiles and laughter and
 Make my life as whole.

6/6/00

MOMENTS SPENT ALONE

*M*oments spent alone
  My thoughts are all of you;
The things we used to share
  I meant so much to you;

*N*ow the times have changed
  And our love has fell apart;
Envisioning days of laughter
  Now I nurse a broken heart;

I could not think to imagine
  That our love was not forever;
Now a past that falls behind me
  Now a new life to endeavor;

*S*peechless at times
  I think, I cry;
Wondering at moments
  If we both could have tried;

*M*oments spent alone
  My thoughts are all of you;
I search inside my soul
  For answers and for truths;

*S*till, I have no answer
  What has torn apart us two;
Knowing that forever
  I'm still in-love with you.

6/23/00

I THOUGHT OF YOU TODAY

I thought of you today
and the time we used to spend;
it's amazing how things have changed;

When you were in my life
I felt like a more complete person;
You made me whole;

When you held me in your arms
I felt safe;
I know it was where I belonged;

Whenever my spirits needed lifting
it was your smile that made me tingle;

I always knew you were the one for me
and I pray that one day we will be together again;

I will always love you
and I will wait for that day;
That moment, that time
you will be my everything.

7/21/2000

CONGRATULATIONS

If I forgot to tell you that
I'm proud of you, I am!
You focused on your inner self,
and finally took a stand;

You map out all your goals
and you designate a plan;
Life can be a struggle
but you finally know you can;

Conquer all the obstacles
and hurdles known to man;
As you endure, I wish you well,
and proud of you; I am!

January 2000

LONELINESS

I am alone it's silent though,
    the noise won't fade away;
Alone I chose for not to be
    I wish a brighter day;

I turn at night and open eyes
    A bottomless pit inside;
I peak to see there's no one there
    I wish to stay and hide;

Thoughts inside I want to talk
    you don't exist at all;
Falling deep, a mountain cliff
    who will catch my fall;

I want to laugh, do tickle me
    and make my day be grand;
I cannot laugh for you're not there
    and no one else that can;

How can they say to be alone
    and be all by yourself;
I've been alone for all my days
    and wish for someone else;

You are alone, you be content
    That's what they say to me;
But they do have somebody else
    to help them fall asleep.

LETTING GO OF LOVE

Letting go of love
a difficult task to achieve;
To turn around and walk away
to not look back and leave;

To give up all the time and love
you invested in just one;
To feel the ache, release the tears
to suffer when they're gone;

It's hard to start out fresh
and you hold a tighter grip;
Let go of all the yesterdays
and start to take your trip;

A mountain that you can't avoid
you must climb it to the top;
Through all the pain and suffering
you must be strong, don't stop;

You'll smile again, you'll laugh again
keep climbing the mountain above
In time, will pass the memories of
your letting go of love.

10/2/00

It's Time To Change

Realizing when, it's time to change
>A moment to move on;
>>Knowing all the feelings of your mate
>>>They're dead, they're gone;

To you they're still the world
>And you love them still as much;
>>But when the time has come you must
>>>Love your self as such;

Let go of all the empty dreams
>And pains of the one that's gone;
>>In search and need of inner strength
>>>Indulge in the Lord, be strong;

Although, it seems impossible
>To make it through a day'
>>Realize that you are not the first
>>>And you will be okay;

Tomorrow will reward you of
>The happiness you need;
>>And though it is a struggle now
>>>Believe you will succeed.

10/04/00

WHEN THE HEART WON'T LET YOU GO

When the heart won't let you go
    So, to free your inner soul;
A moment in time must come
    When to know that love has gone;

The strength must come within
    and you gather all you can;
Also focus on a goal
    For the heart must have its hold;

At times you think you can't
    But you know that you must do;
Look upon the lord
    For he will pull you through;

No storm is that too great
    For the times will change; you wait;
As the sun will follow soon
    Have faith; your happiness will bloom;

In tomorrow you will find
    That today has passed behind;
For your heart has set you free
    For once; at peace you'll surely be.

10/17/00

I Might Say To You I Love You

I might say to you
    I love you;
Darling know this to be true;
    The warmth of tender memories
I am harboring loving you;

A longing to touch my baby

To also caress you ole so tight;
To yearn your warm embrace
As I lay throughout the night;

Emotions that I cannot understand

As they crept into my heart;
The imagining of your beautiful smile
Lifts my spirits when we're apart;

Loving you is simple, sweet

An attraction at its best;
A gift from one above
Our love is surely blessed;

I might say to you
    I love you;
And, my darling,
    I surely do;
An eternity of love
    I wish, of loving you.

10/23/00

FORGETFUL LOVE

I forgot to say the words
The ones I often do;
To tell you that I miss you

    And I'm so in love with you;

It's not that I'm not focused
And it isn't I don't care;
For every time I blink my eye

    I see moments that we share;

Not because I don't
For my love, I always will;
Even during the worst of times

    The love will be there still;

There's no excuse my honey
No explanation dear;
No reason why I did not whisper

    The words you need to hear;

I lacked to give you comfort
I what I didn't do;
Forgot to hug and kiss you

    And to say that I love you.

SORRY FOR THE PAIN

How could I say I love you
yet bring you pain inside your heart;
Make you hurt and make you suffer
and tear our love apart;

How could I hold you closely
lie within your arms at night;
To wake you up in the morning
just to argue and cause fights;

Sending you a message
not once but many times;
One proclaiming you'll find no love
within this heart of mine;

Sending you these signals
displays selfishness in me;
Throwing away a love that's strong
the kind I want and also need;

I'm sorry for the heartache
all the selfish foolish deeds;
For letting you down when all you asked for
was a chance at loving me;

I do not want to loose you
and deep inside I know;
The road ahead gets better
and our love is free to grow.

*K*EEPER *O*F *M*Y *H*EART

*Y*ou tell me to leave,
    You tell me just walk;
I proclaim no baby,
    My honey, let's talk;

*Y*ou say nothings left,
    Nothing for you to say;
My showers and clouds,
    And rainy days;

*F*ollow shortly after I leave,
    As I walk and I turn;
Not a moment of before,
    Not a lesson I've learned;

*Y*ou've said before,
    And meant it true;
My heart pounding deep,
    It's pounding for you;

*M*y world yes you were,
    My everything that I had;
Blinded by the love,
    Now faded now sad;

*H*olding on to my heart,
    As I try to take it back;
Smiling,
    For no love did my heart ever lack;

*T*o keep my love inside deep,
    As to not give away;
The keeper of my heart,
    Will come collecting one day.

11/9/00

DETACHMENT

Hopes, aspirations, wishes and dreams
    It's hard to let you go;
A darkness, a sadness, a tear inside
The feeling one must know;

    Detach, let go
        Don't hold onto me tight;
    To have you but to share you
        It's not completely right;

        Feelings of a loneliness
            I've walked this path before;
        My lord, my father, the one above
            He wished for so much more;

    Climbing on to step ahead
        Seeks strength within my soul;
    I've conquered half a time before
        The notions of a whole;

Detach, let go
    The wonders of something you must do;
A heart inside, within my soul
    A place belongs to you.

I MUST HAVE MORE THAN ONE

Delusional, Master-mind,
 No peace;

That's the way it be's Sometime
My mind, Noooo
 I know what I see's, I know what I know's
 Grows, my heart, deep in love with you, You too, no what a blow;

Tricked into believing you care
 I don't dare, think that you don't;
 You won't, do for me what I do for you
 You love me too?

You dance, you swirl, you flaunt your smile
 All awhile my presence no where to be found;
 III, Me, I love you for what you be, for my heart, you are the keeper of the key;
 My mind running wild;

Sleep today, no neither yesterday;
 It doesn't exist;
 But the memory of your kiss, remains so close, to close, I fiend for a dose
 A hug, the one I can't resist, I persist;
 Holding, tugging, pleading and praying
 All along, my heart so sadly saying;

Love,
 Tough yours repeats, many, and many, and many ladies
 One, no I can have some;
  I must have more than one.

11/13/00

Made in the USA
Middletown, DE
30 May 2022